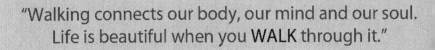

"Walking connects our body, our mind and our soul.
Life is beautiful when you WALK through it."

Risa Olinsky

Dedicated to our husbands,
who brought us together

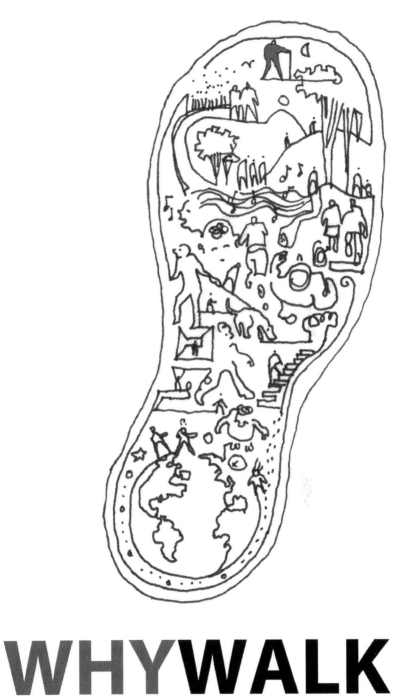

WHYWALK

By Risa Olinsky

Illustrated by Carol Hsiung

Introduction

I grew up on the south shore of Long Island where there were no mountains, though there were great beaches. I knew nothing about hiking or even walking more than a mile or so and, as a child, that was usually a walk to the nearest five-and-dime. Life in the suburbs was more about cars and bicycles. To the adult generation of post WWII, a car was a status symbol. What you drove was important. To a child a bicycle meant freedom, a way of getting around the neighborhood, but very few people simply walked because 1950 Long Island communities were not designed for pedestrians.

My life was pretty normal other than being 30 pounds overweight with a poor body image and a stress-eating problem. I had friends, was a good student and spent a lot of time practicing the piano, but I also loved being active and outdoors as well. My childhood dream was to be a musician. In September of 1973, this dream came true. I was off to Boston University as a music/piano major.

Reality check: To succeed as a pianist, one needed to practice several hours a day – I did.
You'd practice in small cubicle-like rooms in the basement
of an old musty building and no daylight.

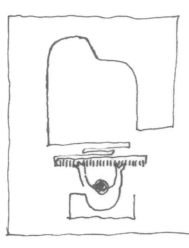

Every time I'd make a mistake I'd grab some loose change
and head to the vending machine for candy or something
to numb my frustration. With this emotional stress and
very little physical activity, things continued to get worse.
The little exercise I'd get was walking to and from my dorm
that was super close to the music school.

Don't get me wrong; I was good. If I hadn't been, I never
would have made it as far as I did, but I was very unhappy.
I thought to myself, just work harder and longer and you
would succeed. The more I worked at it, the unhappier I
became. Something had to change.

Life has a funny way of re-directing you, but it's easy to miss the road signs if you're not paying attention. I missed a few along the way, but this next one came with headlights. I didn't miss it.

Monday, October 14, 1974: I was invited to do something I'd never done before – climb a mountain! Not just any mountain, but Mount Washington in New Hampshire. It was the beginning of my sophomore year. At 5'1" and 155 pounds (yes, I gained the freshman 15), I could hardly walk a flight of steps without getting winded, and I was off to hike Mount Washington.

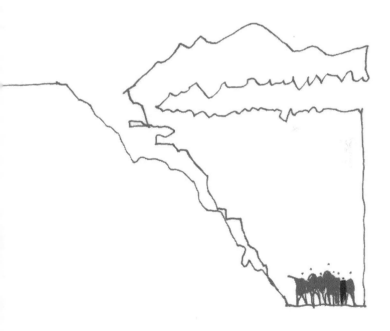

It was a class field trip with a unique focus: a study in healthy lifestyles. Yes, the topic was long before its time. My young and strapping professor led us up the foothills to the jagged rocks higher up. We hiked a decent distance up when a mixture of rain and snow started, so we turned around and headed back down. With muddy and slippery conditions, most of the group managed to stay on their feet coming down, but not me. I didn't have the right clothes or shoes (knew nothing about hiking boots) so I ended up on my butt sliding down the mountain and laughing all the way.

I was soaking wet and cold, and yet my body never felt so good – so alive. It was as though I was breathing life into muscles I didn't know I had. My thoughts and feelings were clearer than they had ever been before, and though I'd been hiking for several hours, I wasn't even hungry. How could this be? I could sit practicing for one hour and be hungry, but not after hours of physical activity.

That day on Mount Washington, I uncovered
a physical person trapped in a sedentary body.

I had to move, not sit.

I had to be outside, not inside a practice room.
It felt as though a fog that had been covering my whole
body was gone. That one day and one hike changed
the direction I would go in. I changed career goals and
school, and moved to New York City, where I'd walk
almost everywhere I could. I'd walk for miles. To keep
from getting bored, I'd count my steps from corner to
corner up to 100 and start over again. This was long
before high-tech gadgets to track steps.

I'd walk to think, to breathe and to take in the city life.
I was young and money was tight. Walking saved
money on transportation. And along with a few other
lifestyle changes, I was losing weight!! Walking became
a kind of friend, something I could depend on being
there when needed.

Walking and the Mind...

Movement has a powerful effect on one's mind,
emotions and thoughts. Imagine your thoughts
are jumbled and emotions spinning around:
take a walk and your head begins to clear.
Tune out and turn off electronics.
Breathe in and out slowly feeling the air filling your lungs.
Our body and our mind are one, connected by our breath.
Have a problem you can't solve?
Walk and the answer may come to you.
I didn't know all this when I was young;
all I knew was that moving felt better than not.
Later on I learned to pay closer attention to what
my body was telling me – move!

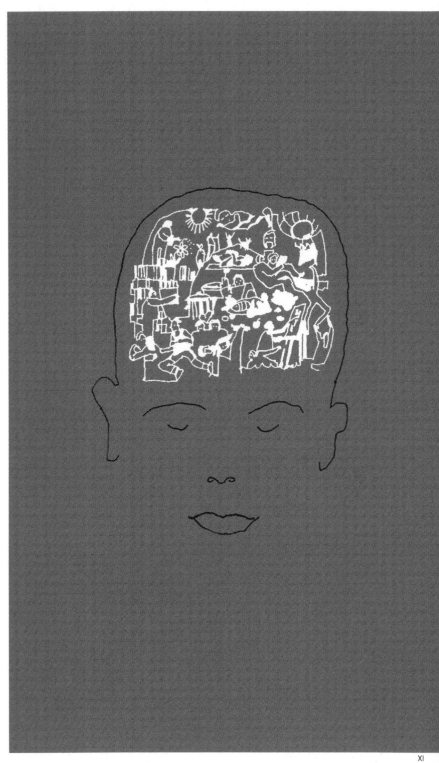

Walking and the Body....

Children move without thinking about why they are
doing it – they just do it.
They move to play, to seek, to find –
to enjoy the ability to walk, to run, to climb.
It's natural; it's what we are meant to do,
but somehow what seems so natural fades away
as life gets more serious.
Children fall, they get up and keep moving;
we fall and fear moving again.
I know. I've been in that dark place.

We park as close as we possibly can to a store.
We drive to the health club to walk on a treadmill.
We build roads without sidewalks, making it that much
more difficult to live without a car.
How can we change this lifestyle?
Find a purpose: a goal,
a reason to be somewhere and walk there.
If your legs work, use them.
If you have limitations, injuries or pain, start slowly,
gradually building your ability to walk longer or farther.

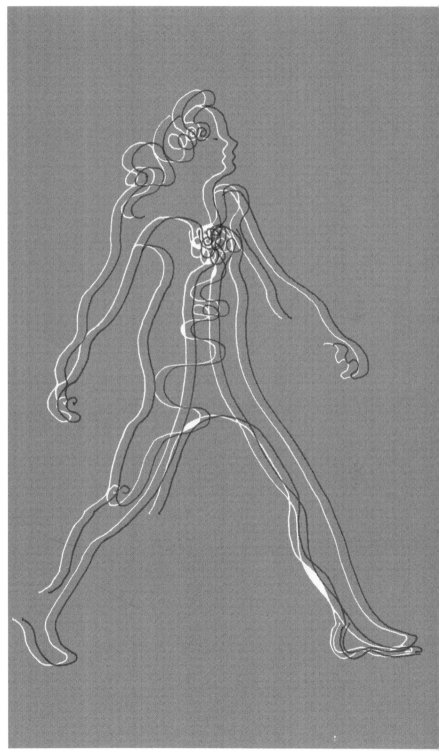

Walking and the Soul....

Why Walk?
Your answer to this question will be the motivation
needed to move you forward.
A parent's heart beats quickly chasing a child
running towards the street.
A young couple walks hand-in-hand on the beach.
A soldier runs from gunfire on the battlefield to safety.
A grandmother back in the 1920's walked to the store
to buy food for her family.
Walking or running, it's all the same. It's what we do;
it's what we are meant to be doing.

Newborns are carried or pushed in a stroller.
It's universal that at around a year old, children take
their first few steps, opening up the world to explore
by walking. Later in life we may walk with a cane
or the aid of a walker on wheels. To a senior the ability
to walk equals a sense of independence.
Ultimately, we may be in a wheelchair, again pushed
as we started life in a stroller.
The cycle of life begins with learning to walk....
How easy it is to take walking for granted.

Walking connects our body, our mind and our soul.
Life is beautiful when you WALK through it.

WHY WALK is a collage of voices. Not anyone in particular,
not male or female, but universal - a collection of
motivational thoughts and life experiences.

Why Walk? Because you can...

I polled hundreds of people
around the world and asked...

WHY WALK?

Here's what I learned...

"When I walk, the child in me comes out.
I smile.
I laugh.
I feel joy.
I remember the days growing up
when I'd walk to the five-and-dime
to buy bubble gum.
Now I walk and stop for coffee."

"I walk to reduce my carbon footprint.
The environment is important to me.

I gave up my car and walk
or take public transporation
to get to where I need to go."

"I walk to ward off
my family's history
of heart disease.
My father died of a massive
heart attack when I was 10;
he was only 45.

He never got to see me grow up -
I miss him terribly.
I just turned 40.
My wife and I
are having our first baby.
I want to be around to see
our child grow up."

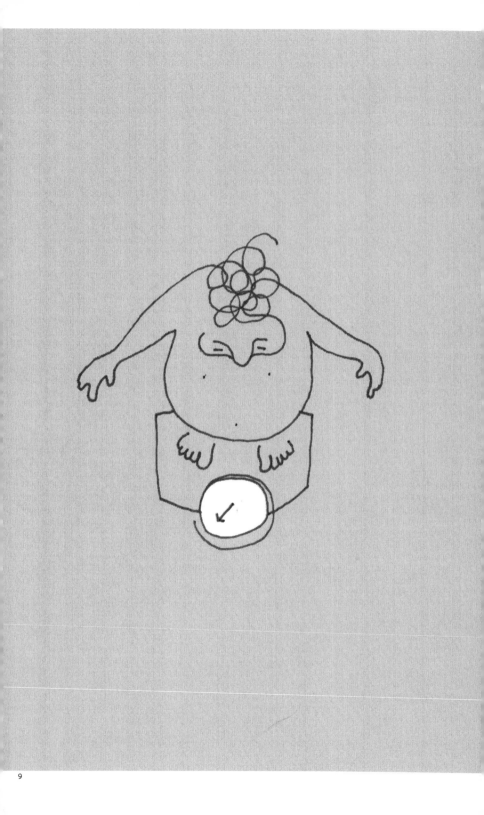

"I walk so I won't gain back the weight
I lost after lap-band surgery."

"I wore out my knees running.
I'm blessed with two new knees.
No more running for me.

Instead, I've taken up long-distance walking
and I **LOVE** it!"

"I walk because one night,
after a few too many drinks,
I ran my car off the road and nearly killed
someone.
Thankfully, they lived.
My life changed that night.
I've given up both driving
and drinking completely.
Now, I walk whenever I possibly can
and take public transportation
when needed.
I'm healthier
and others are better off
with me off the road."

"I walk to feel the seasons --
the hot,
the cold,
the sun and the rain.
I walk in all kinds of weather."

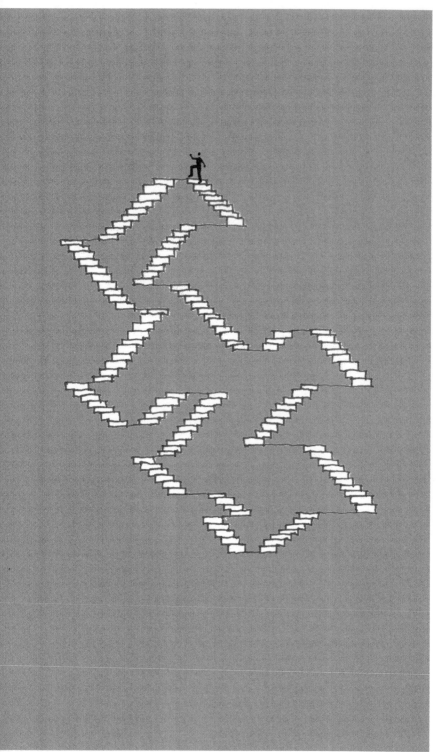

"I am 50 years old, severely obese
and live hooked up to oxygen most days.
Feeling hopeless after years of trying numerous
weight loss and exercise programs,
I turned to a health coach for help.
She set me up with a simple pedometer
to monitor my daily steps.
Day one the pedometer read 500 steps.

Together, we discussed what would be
a reasonable goal. I said that I would add
100 steps a day for the next week.
By the end of the week,
I achieved my goal of 1,200 steps in one day.

One month later, I was able to walk
short distances outside without oxygen
averaging 2,000 steps a day.
To some, this may not sound like much,
but to me it was huge.

On days I feel discouraged,
I remind myself that every step counts."

"I walk to take deep breaths.
It helps me manage the anxiety I live with.
Walking gives me a sense of peace
in a fast-paced and stressful world."

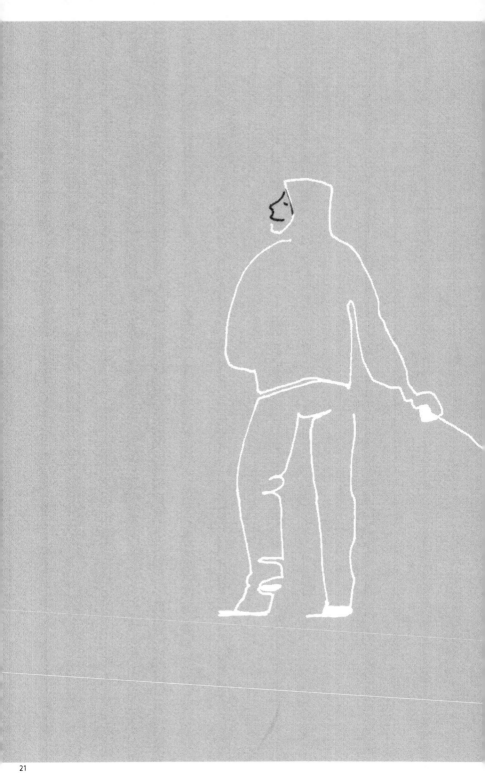

"My dog is sick
and needs to pee a lot.
I wouldn't be walking as much
if not for him.

Once outside, I feel like
I needed the walk
as much or more than my dog."

"I walk on weekends.
I have a sedentary job
with long hours during the week,
and though it's just two days,
it's better than nothing -
right?"

"I walk to socialize.
I'm not so self-motivated to go by myself,
but if a friend calls,
I'm dressed and ready in minutes
to hit the road together."

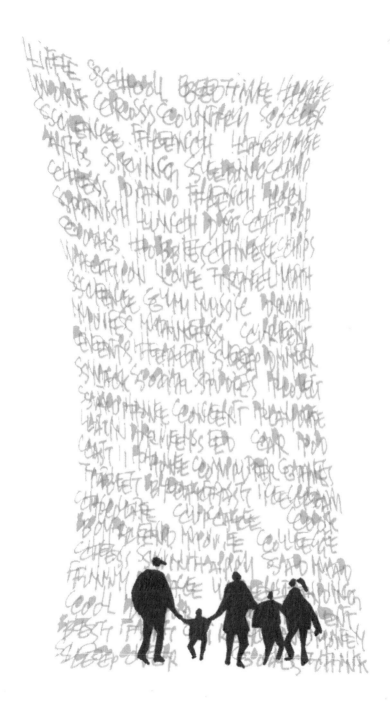

"My husband and I were overweight
and sedentary children.
We take family walks
to set an example for our kids.
It's a great time to talk to them
about everything and anything.

Our hope
is that they will enjoy being active
and, in turn,
not struggle with their weight
like we did at their age."

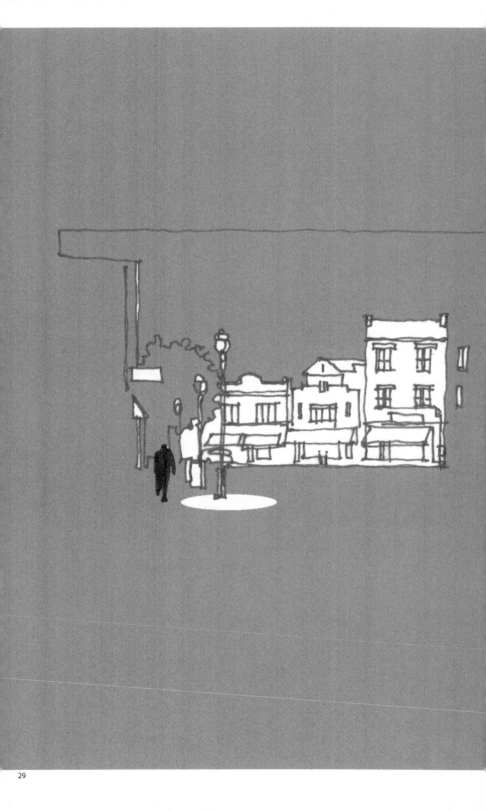

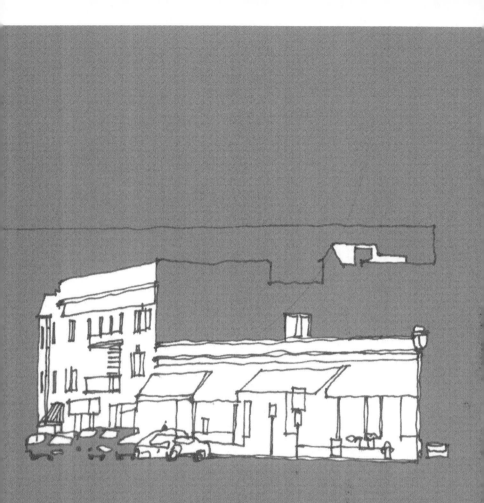

"I walk in the evening after dinner.
It's relaxing and helps digest my food."

"I own a business.
If I need to meet with someone,
I invite them to walk with me instead of
talking by phone or sitting in an office.

It gets me off my butt,
helps me focus
and sets an example for others.

I encourage my employees
to do the same when possible."

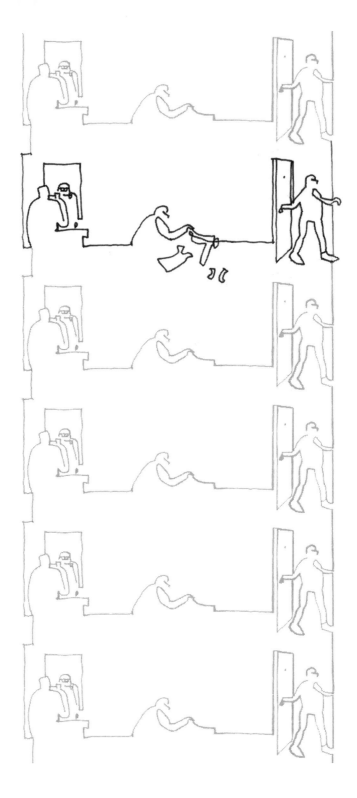

"My daily two-mile walk
is like brushing my teeth -
a habit.

I lay out my clothes the night before,
get up,
get dressed
and head out the door
without thinking twice."

"I've had some personal health issues.
Walking gets me going
in more ways than one."

"I used to take a pill.

Now I walk instead.
Things are looking up!"

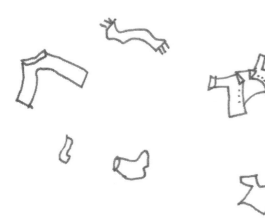

"I walk my twins in a stroller at naptime.
They love the fresh air
and fall right to sleep.

The added bonus is,
I get to move.

Some afternoons,
we can be out walking
for up to two hours."

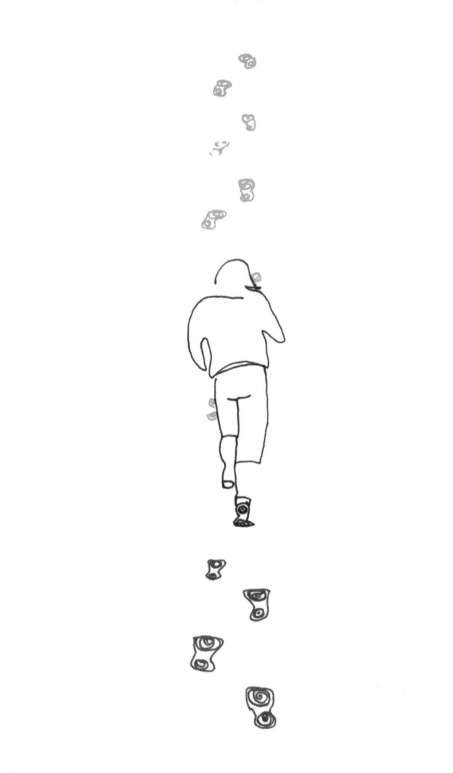

"I walk as a personal challenge.
At first, walking three miles a day felt like a lot,
then suddenly it was easy,
so I started adding a bit more each day.
Now, I can walk close to ten miles in ONE day.
I never imagined this even possible.
Time to set a new goal!"

"I walk and talk
on the phone.
I catch up with
friends and family
and keep moving
at the same time.

Who said multi-tasking isn't productive?"

"I walk to keep my skin
healthy and clear.
I suffer with acne
that gets worse
when I am stressed.

When I maintain a
walking routine my skin improves.
Stress hurts and walking helps.
When my skin looks good,
I feel good."

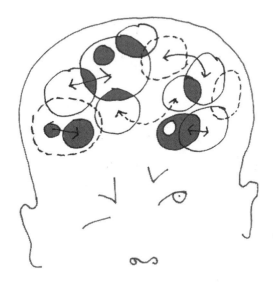

"I walk to think through problems
and manage my life."

"I have terminal cancer.
I've accepted that I don't know
how long I have to live.
Walking helps me focus on living,
not dying."

"I walk on the beach.
I have asthma, so breathing in the salt air
feels really good."

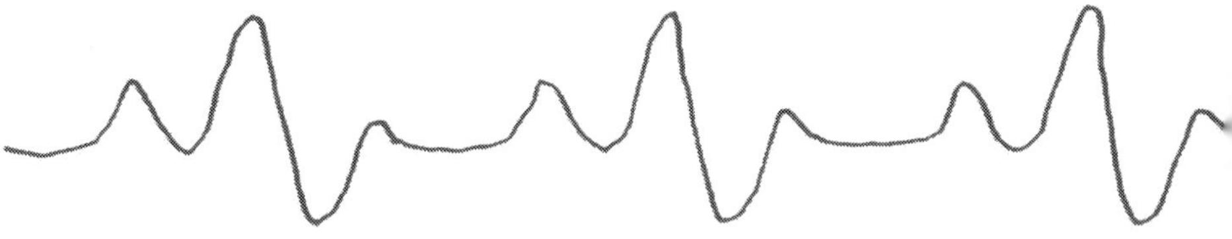

"I walk because at 60
I was fortunate enough to get a new heart.
My doctor's instructions
were to **use it**."

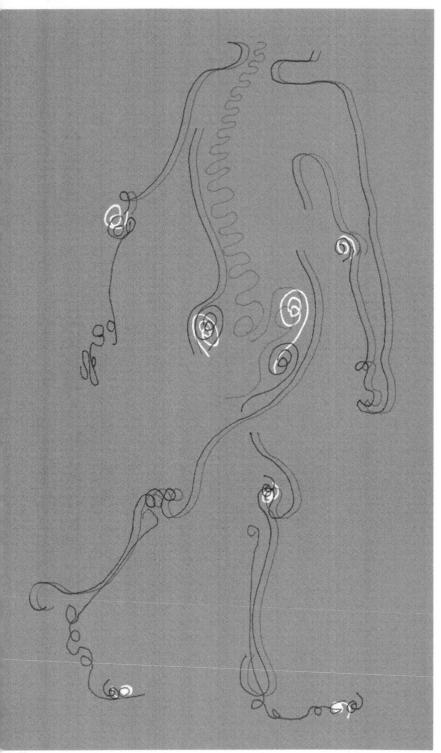

"I walk to keep degenerative arthritis
from taking over my body.
It hurts to move,
but hurts more when I don't."

"I walk for many reasons,
but most importantly
to spend quality time with my adult son,
brain-injured in an accident.

I have a high-power and stressful job
that supports our family, but
I wouldn't miss our walks together
for the world."

"I love to walk and
meet folks along the way.
I learn about their lives.
Occasionally, we sit down and rest
and then walk some more.
I've listened to some amazing life stories."

"I walk because sometimes
I need to be alone
and have a good cry.
It's cathartic, no one sees me
and when I get back home,
I'm fine."

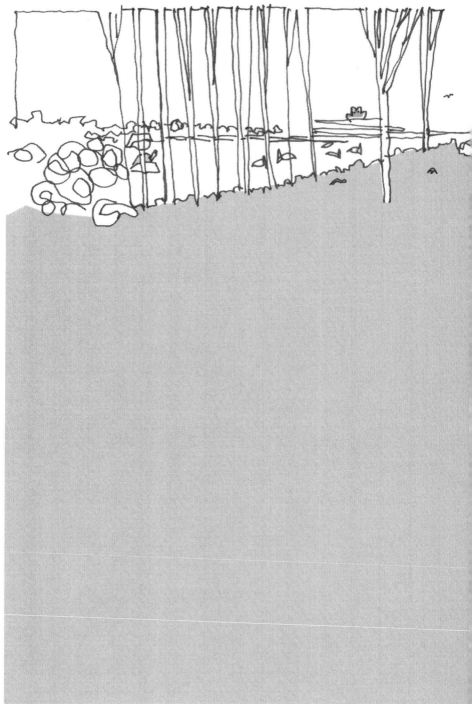

"I walk because I see really cool things
along the way,
things I would surely miss
if I were in a car or on a bicycle."

"I love to travel.
Everywhere I go, I walk.
Walking gives me an up-close
and personal view of the place I'm in."

"My 60 year-old mother was recently
diagnosed with stage four breast cancer.
I felt hopeless,
so I organized a few friends,
which then became a larger group
to raise money by walking for the cause.

That was three years ago.
My mother has since passed away,
but every year I still walk in her memory,
and for my own health as well."

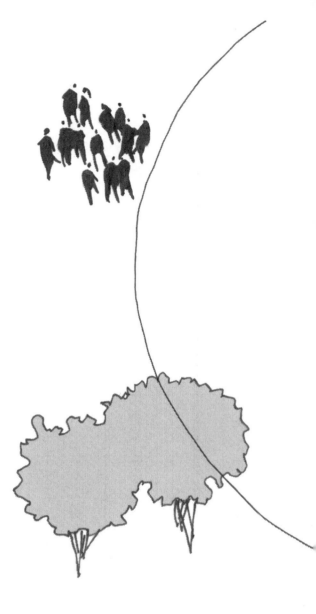

"I'm divorced.
I'm lonely.
I walk in organized groups
to be with people
without feeling like a third wheel."

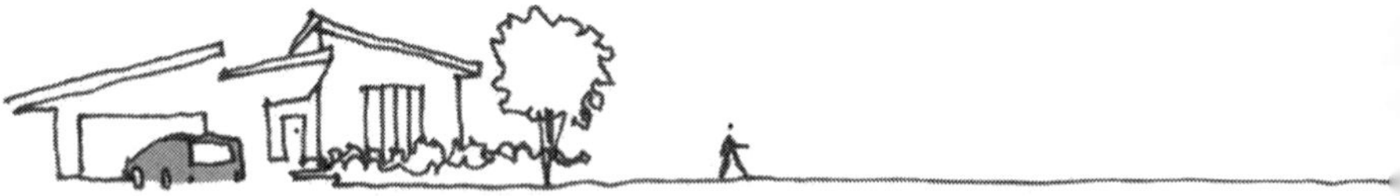

"I live on a really tight budget.
I walk to save money
on gas and parking.
I do own a car and drive
only when I really need to."

"I walk to reconnect
with the beauty of the world.

It awakens gratitude, which
brings me closer to God."

"I walk very slowly,
but thankful I'm still on my feet.
A car hit me.
My legs were badly broken.

The doctors put me back together again,
a bit like Humpty Dumpty.

I'm on disability and can't do much,
but I can walk slowly.
Eventually, I get where I need to be."

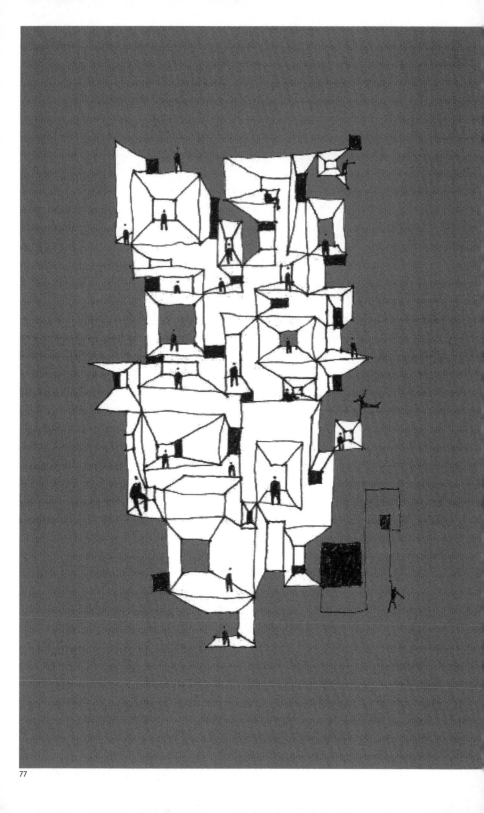

"I walk away the demons....
to empty my mind."

"I love good food,
no apologies.
At times I indulge a bit more than planned.
I walk so I can enjoy my food:
calories in, calories out.

Is it a perfect science?
No, but it's working for me,
so I'll keep walking and eating,
or should I say
eating and walking?"

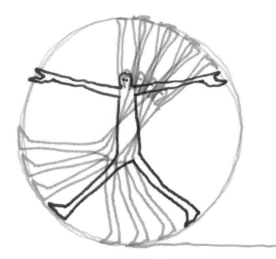

"I walk because I don't have a job.
I can't afford health club fees
or exercise equipment.

Walking is **free!**"

"I walk with my wife
who needs the exercise
but is scared to go alone,
so we go together.

A win-win for us both."

"I walk to pray.
I don't need the confined walls
of a building to help me
connect with my spirit.

All I need is open space
and personal time."

"I walk to be a powerful
and confident woman.
I'm 30 years-old.
Last summer I was mugged
walking to a train station.
Thankfully I wasn't hurt.
This was scary
but it will not stop me
from walking."

"I was born with scoliosis –
a crooked spine.
As a child, my doctors advised me
to stay active so my muscles
would support my spine.
I didn't listen back then… now I do.

For the past 40 years I've led an active life -
walking and working out.

Now, I'm in my 60s and the doctors say,
'whatever you are doing, keep doing it.'"

"When I am alone on a path,
I walk and sing along
with the music in my ears -
like karaoke.

One day walking on a quiet road,
thinking I was alone,
someone came up to me and said,
'How nice to hear someone singing.'
I said, 'Thank you,'
and continued walking and singing...
with a smile on my face."

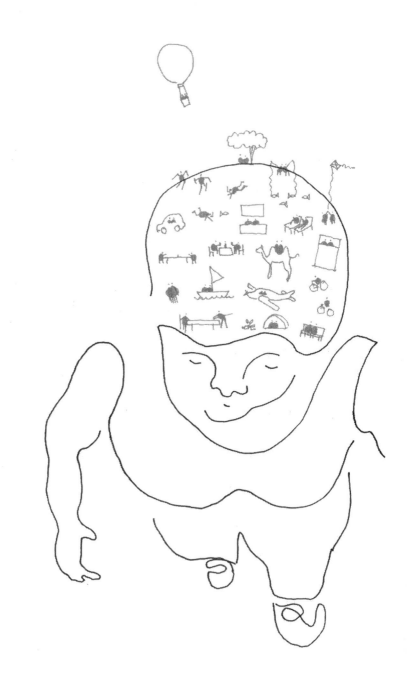

" I started walking in my late 60s
after I lost my husband.
We were married 45 years.
We recently retired
and looked forward
to enjoying the good life
We were happy.

He died of a sudden heart attack,
no warning.
We were both overweight.
It didn't mattter to either of us.

It matters to me now,
but it can't bring my husband back.
I've lost a lot weight.
I wish we had started walking sooner."

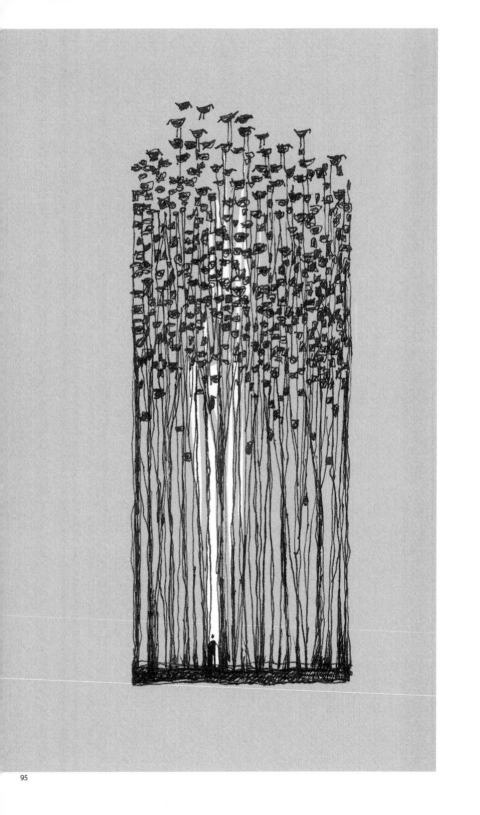

"I live with depression.
I walk to avoid medication."

"I walk to wear out my dog
so he'll sleep
and not bark at the kids
coming home from school at 3 PM."

"I walk because my last colonoscopy was a bit scary; I want to reduce my risk of cancer."

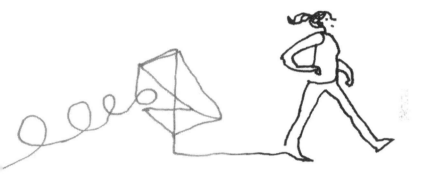

"It's simple.
I can't run.
I'm terrified of the water.
I don't ride a bike
and never learned a sport.

Walking is the only way
I can get regular exercise.
That's it, done deal."

"In my mid 50s life changed,
my numbers started going up and up:
increased weight,
blood pressure,
glucose,
cholesterol and heart rate -
the whole package.
I needed to do something.

I joined a women's walking group.
We've been walking together for six months.
My numbers have come down
within normal range.

My friends and I kvetch
about our aches and pains,
and have fun doing it...together."

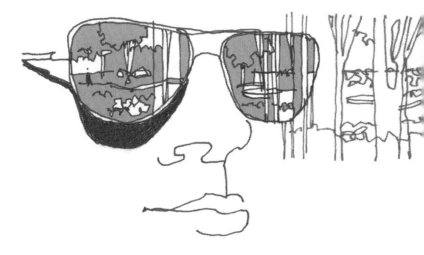

"I walk to enjoy the gardens
in my neighborhod
and get new ideas for improving mine.
Flowers brighten my day."

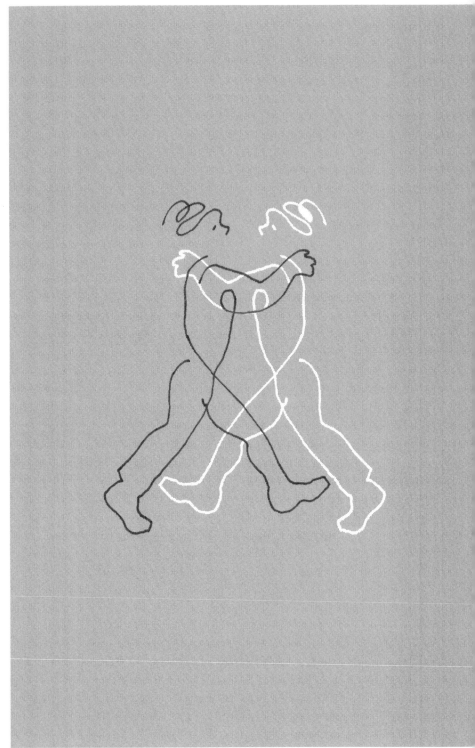

"I walk because I love my body,
and when I do, my body loves me back."

"I walk to feel the ground
under my feet,
the air in my nostrils
and the sun on my skin.

I walk slowly to enjoy
the sensations that abound."

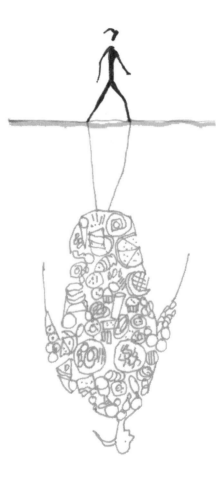

"I walk to keep tabs on a
life-long eating disorder.
Sometimes, I just feel out of control,
binge on whatever is around,
and then throw up.

Yes, it's really gross and every time I do it,
I hate myself for it.

I'm in therapy and working on it.
Meanwhile, walking and getting away
from food gives me a
sense of control and peace."

"I walk to do errands.
It takes more time,
but I am getting my exercise
while getting things done."

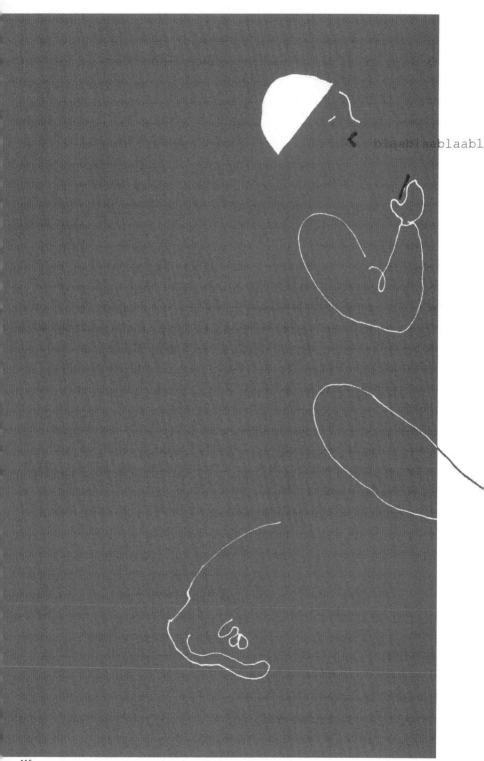

blaablaablaabl

ablaablaablaablaablaablaablaablaablaablaablaa

"I walk to write.
Crazy?

I'm most creative when I am moving.
My thoughts and ideas
become clearer when I walk.
I record my thoughts and type them up
when I get home."

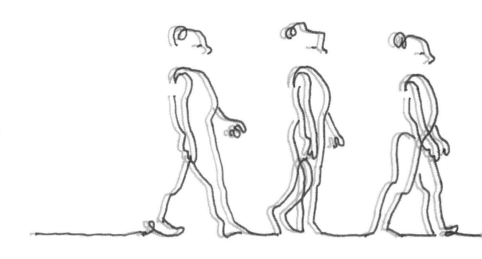

"I walk because I'm getting older.
Walking helps me feel
young and vibrant."

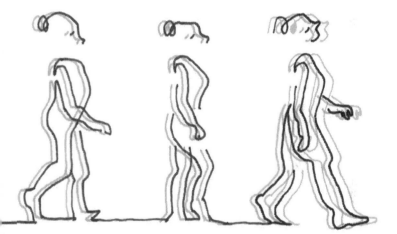

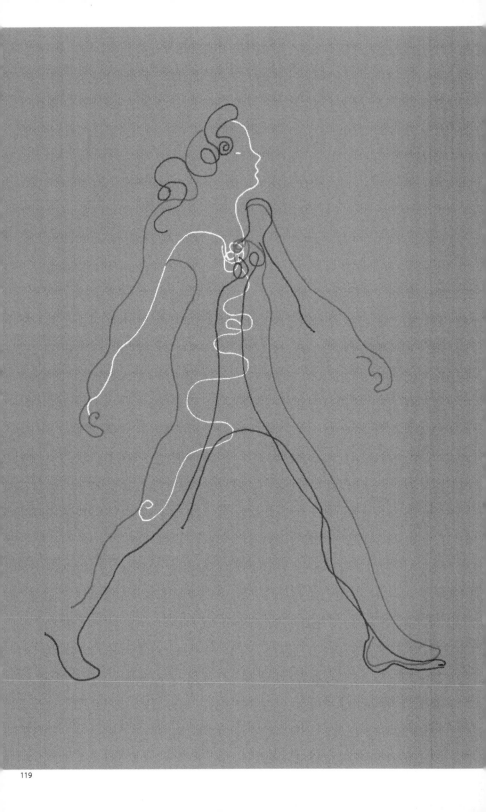

"I was told that high blood pressure
runs in my family.

I started working out in college.
Now, I walk.
My blood pressure is normal.

It's that simple."

"I thought walking might help me lose a
few pounds and fit into my old jeans.

As I increased the days and miles I walked,
I experienced fewer monthly
mood swings and cramps...
you know what I mean.

Wow - this was pretty cool.
Feeling better is a bonus, and yes,
I'm down a size in my jeans...."

"I used to drive a mile once a week
to meet a friend for breakfast.
I'd have coffee, pancakes, eggs and bacon.
I had no energy, and my blood chemistry levels
were horrendous.

Now, I walk the same mile to meet my friend.
I order poached eggs, whole grain toast,
lettuce, tomato and coffee.
After breakfast, I walk home.

I've lost five pounds in a month
and increased my energy.
I'm so proud of myself
that everything in my life has changed.

Next, I hope to convince
my friend to do the same."

"I walk to stay in touch
with a dear friend
who moved away.
We used to walk here in town,
but now
we walk and talk by phone.
We set the date,
time and length of our walk.

Our friendship continues to grow..."

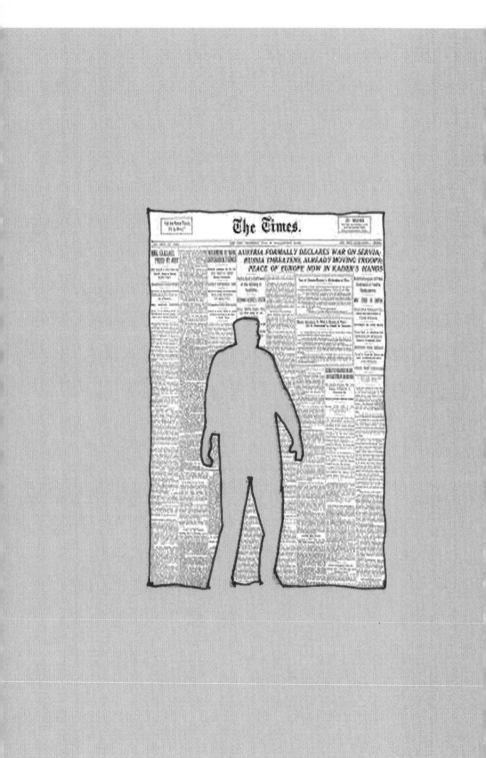

"I walk to escape the noise of the world."

"I lost 30 pounds by sticking
to a daily 5K walking program.

As a result, my medical insurance premiums
dropped considerably.
In addition, since I've been driving fewer miles,
I'm saving on car insurance as well.

What a great 'return on my investment'."

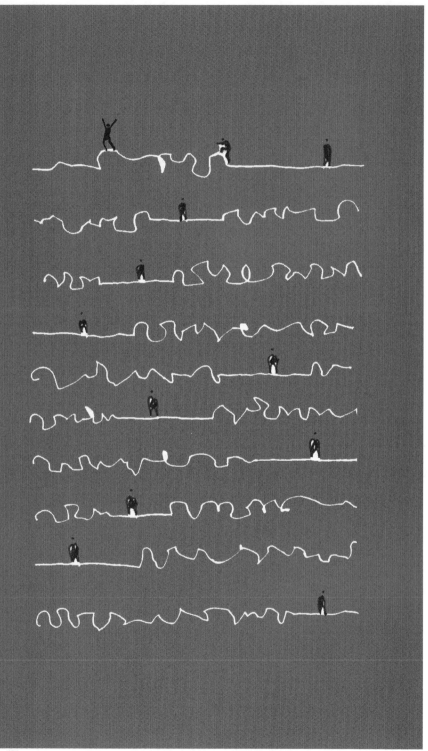

"I walk to boost my confidence. Setting a walking goal and reaching it empowers me to face other challenges in my life."

"I walk not to smoke.

I quit a few months ago,
and I don't want to slide backwards.

Cigarettes are damn expensive.
With the money I'm saving
and the milleage I am walking,
I will be physically fit
and financially set
to take a fabulous walking vacation."

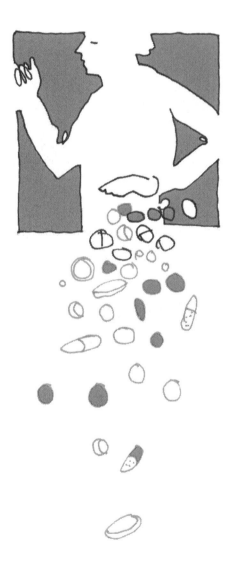

"I walk because every time I go to a doctor
with various aches and pains,
he takes out his Rx pad
and starts writing prescriptions for me.

I don't want pills.
I just want to feel better.

Walking has been the best medicine yet."

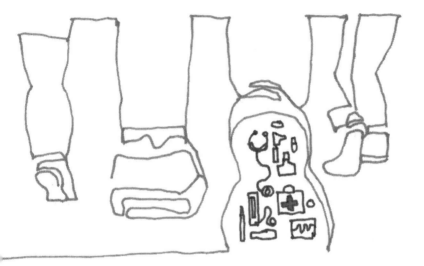

"I walk to take responsibility for my health
and not rely on the insurance company
or the government to pay
for unneccessary health care costs
that could be avoided
if I take control of my health."

"I walk to recharge
my internal batteries."

"I walk to stay sober."

"I go on 'historical' walking tours.
The leaders tell stories
about the places we're walking through.
It's like going back in time
and a lot more fun than sitting
and reading about these places.

I'm exercising my brain
and my body together."

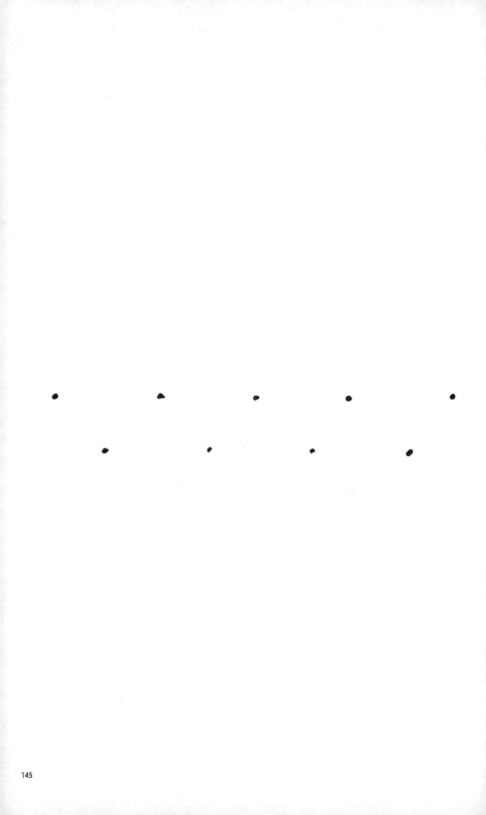

"I walk with trekking poles.
People think poles are for those
who can't walk without them - not so.

The poles enable me
to do more challenging walks.

I love walking with my poles."

"I'm 87 years old.
I've been walking daily for most of my life.
I still walk about 10 minutes a day.

I can get up and down
from a chair with ease,
compared to some of my friends
who aren't as active as me.

Walking gives me a sense
of continued independence.
I know I'm fortunate
to be able to do what I do at my age.
I don't take it for granted."

"My husband and I live
in an amazing community
where walking is a way of life.
We walk to stores,
to movies, to restaurants
and more.

There's a new buzzword
- walkability -
used to rate how walkable
a community is.

I'm glad I live in a place where others walk,
so I'm motivated to do so as well."

"I walk long distances -
not just for the physical challenge-
but for a delicious adventure
that touches the human spirit.
It's about the people you meet along the way.
It's about crossing over a bridge
to spy a magnificent waterfall,
or turning a corner
and discovering a quaint, old-world village.
It's about passing someone's front porch
and hearing a voice shout out to you,
'And, what are you walking for?'
You reply,
'for fun and my health and just because...'
They smile back and reply..
'Wow, that's great.'

They might wake up tomorrow and
say to themselves, 'I can do that,'
and start walking too
JUST for FUN!"

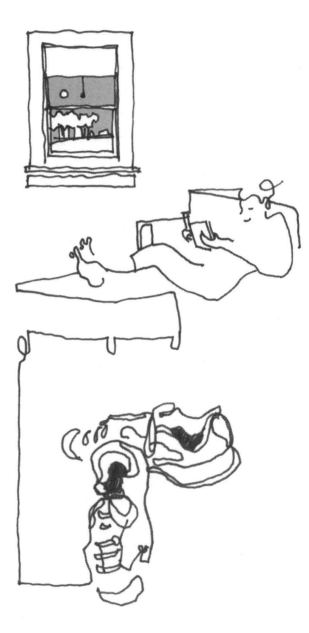

"I walk because after I walk,
I feel great!"

"I walk simply because I can,
and if the day comes that I can't,
I will be grateful that I did while I could."

Risa Olinsky

Risa Olinsky writes about the simple joys of walking through one's life. Managing life-long scoliosis and degenerative arthritis and having had several orthopedic surgeries, now in her 60s, she continues to walk several miles a day. As a walk leader with FreeWalkers, a charitable non-profit organization, Risa does what some might call "extreme" walks of 30-plus miles in one day. She's been a classical pianist, dancer/actor and in the early 1980's went back to school for her graduate degree in health and fitness. As a young woman, she overcame her own health-related challenges and for 35 years has continued helping others do so as well. Risa lives in Maplewood, New Jersey, a wonderfully walkable community, with her husband Mark and their cat Yoohoo. **WHY WALK** is Risa's first full-length book, one of more to come.

"As we age, things will hurt.
I'll take the aches and pains of being active,
versus those of not."

Risa Olinsky

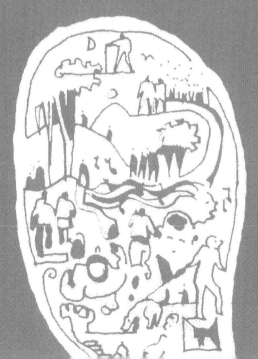

Carol Hsiung is an architect, a published artist and an avid sketcher who loves to create stories with her drawings. She currently lives in New Jersey with her husband and son where they spend a lot of time walking their dog.

I would like to thank my parents who taught me as a child the joy of walking and my family and friends for their encouragement and support. Special thanks to Robert Hsiung, Bob Hsiung and Tina for their insightful graphic suggestions and ideas. I am very grateful to my husband who introduced me to Risa and to her inspiring world of walking where her words and my drawings could meet in such joyful collaboration.

-Carol Hsiung

Acknowledgements

I'm a moving person; I'm not good at sitting still for long periods of time. Perhaps it's one of the reasons, as you read in the beginning of this book, that I gave up my music career. Writing was not something I imagined myself doing later in life, but after the joy of writing a series of blogs for The New York Times, I thought, "Wow, if I can sit still long enough, I can actually do this!" I thank Tina Kelley and Mary Ann Giordano, both former editors at The New York Times for believing I could write. I've learned that a book is more than one person's words - it's a collaboration inspired and supported by many. With this, I want to express my appreciation to many who may not even realize how they contributed to helping bring **WHY WALK** to life.

Thank you...

First, to my husband, first editor and love of my life, Mark Olinsky. Mark and I met at the New York Health & Racquet Club in 1981. I was a dancer and fitness instructor and he a member and young lawyer. Mark overheard me describing my anxiety about writing my graduate school application essay; at that time writing was not my personal strength. He graciously offered to help and the rest is history as we have been together ever since.

My deepest gratitude to my illustrator, Carol Hsiung: We met through our husbands' close friendship and shared passion for cycling. Though I knew Carol loved to draw, it wasn't until we sat for hours over coffee and discussed this project that it clicked. **WHY WALK** would not be what it is without Carol's spirit, energy and amazing talent. We talk and think at the same speed and on the same plane – we get each other.

Friends and Family...

Thank you David Ascher for challenging me with, "Hey, hotshot, you love to walk, what do you think of walking 50 miles in one day?" That was my first FreeWalkers event and though I didn't make 50, I did walk more miles that day than ever before. FreeWalkers, founded by Paul Kiczek, is a non-profit organization dedicated to promoting long-distance walking. When you spend an entire day, sometimes up to 12 hours, walking with people, you get to know them pretty well. Thank you to my FreeWalker friends – there are far too many to mention, but you all know who you are, and how important you are to me. Thank you Paul for creating an organization that changes lives with every step.

Thank you to my close friends who before moving out of state would join me to walk in all weather and all times of the day: Liz LeClair, Amy Hebard, and Ilene Silver. You've moved, but our motivation and friendship stay alive as we walk and talk together by phone. Thank you to my local friends and neighbors, who smile when they see me walking, wave and ask, "How many miles today?" I'm thankful I live in a walkable community.

Thank you Adriane Berg, dear friend and former client, for sharing your expert tips on writing, publishing and marketing. Special thanks to Susan and Fred Profeta, Danielle Perrotta and Filomena Yarussi for reviewing the book in its various stages and giving us your valuable feedback. Thank you Joel Fotinos for your advice, both as a publisher and an author with first-hand experience in self-publishing.

Annette Steinberg, my mom, Ruth Olinsky, my mother-in-law, and Dorothy Love Brunswick, a life-long friend: three strong women, who, each in their own way have inspired me to follow my dreams wherever they would lead me.

Lastly, my sons, Benjamin and Daniel, who may not share my passion for long distance walking, but do humor me when I say, "Hey guys, I'm out the door at 6 AM tomorrow for a 30-mile walk." I know they're proud of their crazy Mom in her 60s, who just wants to keep moving. Wherever life takes you, I know you will keep moving too!

-Risa Olinsky

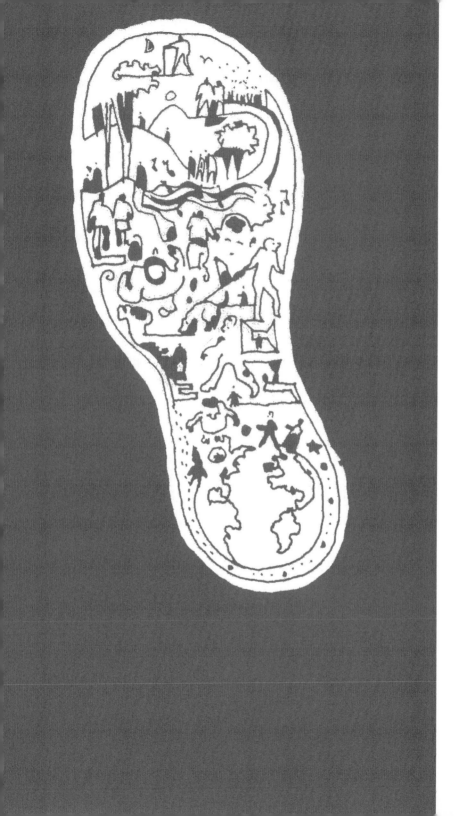

Made in the USA
Middletown, DE
21 April 2018